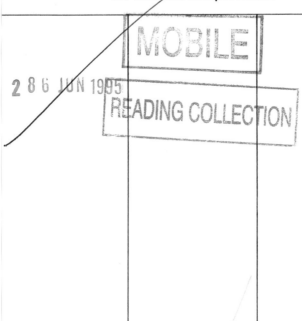

For George

First published 1989 by
Julia MacRae Books
This edition published 1991 by
Walker Books Ltd, 87 Vauxhall Walk
London SE11 5HJ

© 1989 Carol Thompson
Reprinted 1992, 1993

Printed and bound in Hong Kong by
Sheck Wah Tong Printing Press Ltd

British Library Cataloguing in Publication Data
A catalogue record for this book is
available from the British Library.
ISBN 0-7445-1481-9

IN MY
BATHROOM

Carol Thompson

WALKER BOOKS
LONDON

In my bathroom I can
find all sorts of things

a mirror

a bath mat

a tap

a toy

I go to the toilet

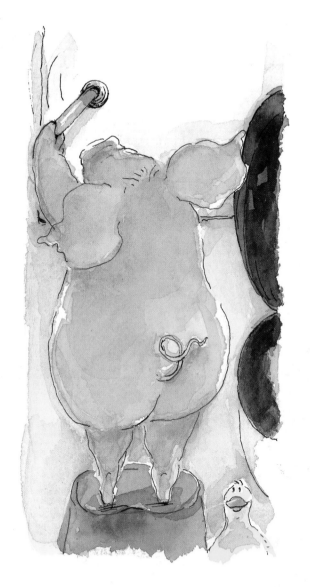

I use the
toilet roll

and pull the
handle

I have my bath

with my soap

my sponge

and my duck

I dry myself

with my towel

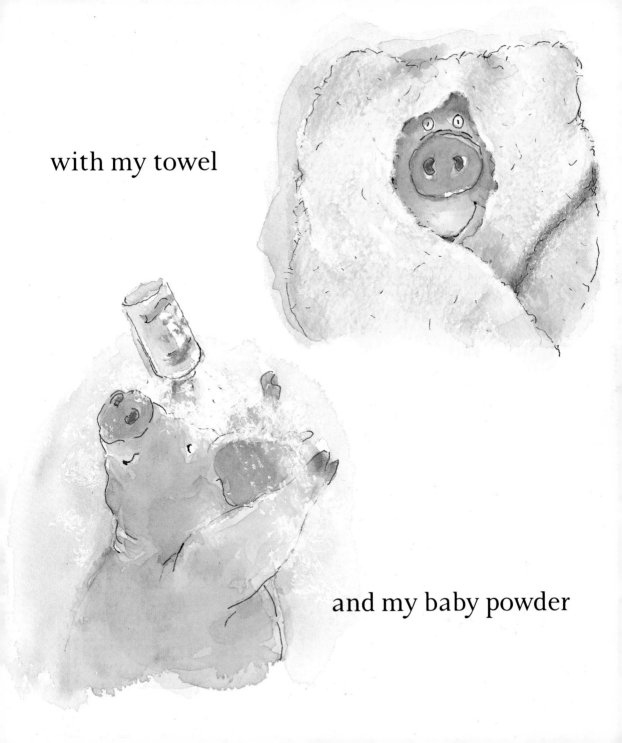

and my baby powder

I clean my teeth

with my tooth-brush

and toothpaste

I brush my hair

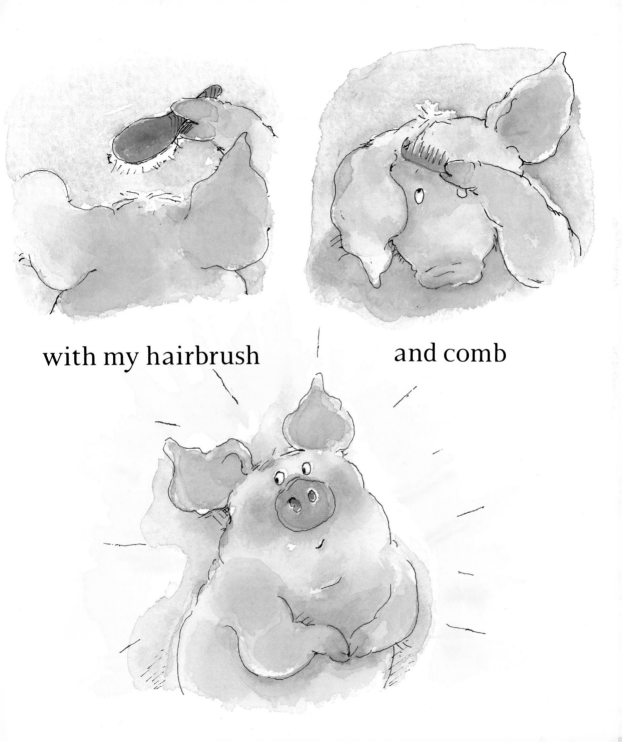

with my hairbrush   and comb

I weigh myself

on my bathroom scales

I get dressed for bed in
my pyjamas and dressing gown

and I go to bed
clean and tidy!

MORE WALKER PAPERBACKS
For You to Enjoy

FARMYARD SOUNDS/JUNGLE SOUNDS
by Colin and Jacqui Hawkins

Animal-sound fun for the very young – everything from a sheep to a snake!

"Children seem unanimous in their liking for the Hawkins' sense of humour and cartoon style pictures." *Books For Keeps*

Farmyard Sounds   ISBN 0-7445-1752-4
Jungle Sounds   ISBN 0-7445-1753-2
£2.99 each

POG
by Peter Haswell

When you look in the mirror, who is it you see there?
What does a banana do? Can you smell a piano? When it comes to
upside-down thinking, there's no one quite like Pog!

"Like a breath of fresh air… My five-year-old found
Pog's antics an absolute hoot." *Esther Ripley, Mother Magazine*

ISBN 0-7445-1766-4   £3.50

**Walker Paperbacks are available from most booksellers, or by post from
Walker Books Ltd, PO Box 11, Falmouth, Cornwall TR10 9EN.**

To order, send: Title, author, ISBN number and price for each book ordered
Your full name and address
Cheque or postal order for the total amount, plus postage and packing:
UK and BFPO Customers – £1.00 for first book, plus 50p for the second book and plus 30p for
each additional book to a maximum charge of £3.00.
Overseas and Eire Customers – £2.00 for first book, plus £1.00 for the second book and
plus 50p per copy for each additional book.
Prices are correct at time of going to press, but are subject to change without notice.